THE STORY OF ANNE FRANK

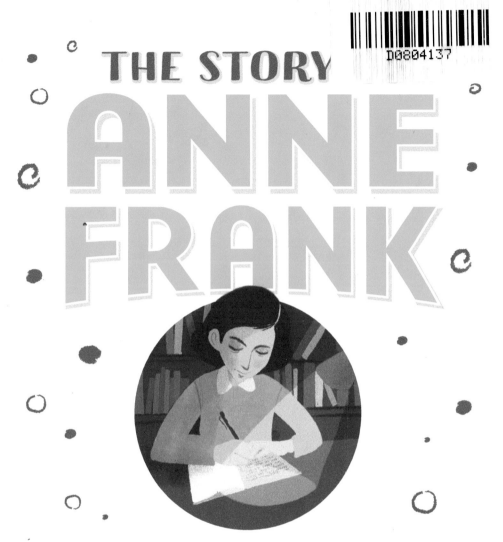

A Biography Book for New Readers

— Written by —
Emma Carlson Berne

— Illustrated by —
Annita Soble

ROCKRIDGE PRESS

For Leo, my creative spark

Series Designer: Angela Navarra

Interior and Cover Designer: Lindsey Dekker

Art Producer: Sara Feinstein

Editors: Orli Zuravicky and Erum Khan

Production Manager: Holly Haydash

Production Editor: Sigi Nacson

Illustrations © 2021 Annita Soble
Photography used under license from Alamy. Author photo courtesy of Amanda Sheehan.

ISBN: Print 978-1-64876-606-0 | Ebook 978-1-64739-896-5

R0

CONTENTS

CHAPTER 1

A DREAMER IS BORN

❦ Meet Anne Frank ❧

Anne Frank was born with a very active imagination. Sometimes, Anne spent the night at her friend's house next door. She always brought an empty suitcase with her, because she didn't feel like she was *really* traveling unless she had a suitcase.

Anne had long brown hair that she loved to brush. She liked fancy clothes, movie stars, and attention. She also liked to think and read. She wanted to be a writer when she grew up.

Anne lived in the Netherlands, in the city of Amsterdam, during **World War II**. She died in the **Holocaust** when she was only fifteen years old. She was killed because she was **Jewish**.

Between the years of 1941 and 1945, the German leader Adolf Hitler killed six million Jewish people across Europe. Hitler wanted to be the most powerful ruler of all the countries in Europe. He hated Jews and didn't want Jewish people to exist.

Anne and her family spent two years hiding from Hitler's soldiers, known as the Schutzstaffel, or **SS**, and the **Gestapo**. While she was hiding, Anne wrote down her feelings and thoughts in a special diary. Even though she was suffering, Anne wrote about hope and love. She lived in a world full of hate, but Anne believed that people were still good and that a better world would come soon.

Anne isn't alive today, but her words are saved in her diary. Kids all over the world read Anne's diary. They learn about what it was like to be a Jewish kid during World War II. They also learn that even when terrible things are happening, you don't have to give up hope.

❧ Anne's World ❧

Anne was born on June 12, 1929, in Frankfurt, Germany. She lived with her older sister, Margot, and her parents, Otto and Edith, in an apartment with a little yard and lots of room for books.

Otto was a businessman. His family, like many Jewish families, had lived in Germany for generations. Around the time when Anne was born, Germany was still recovering from losing **World War I**. This massive world war had lasted four years, taken several million lives, and cost the country a lot of money. German people were losing their jobs. They were angry. They felt that they had been treated unfairly after the war.

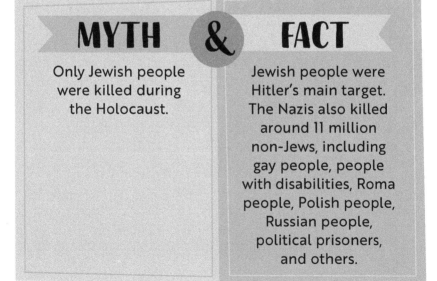

MYTH & FACT

Only Jewish people were killed during the Holocaust.

Jewish people were Hitler's main target. The Nazis also killed around 11 million non-Jews, including gay people, people with disabilities, Roma people, Polish people, Russian people, political prisoners, and others.

Some German leaders blamed the Jewish
people for these problems and announced that
to German citizens. One of these leaders was
Adolf Hitler. He led a **political** group called the
National Socialist German Workers' Party—also
known as the Nazi Party. In 1925, Adolf Hitler
published a book called *Mein Kampf* (mahyn
KAHMPF), which is German for "My Struggle."
The book stated that all Jews should be killed
or removed from society. Hitler wrote that

the world should have killed the Jews during World War I.

This hatred toward Jews is called **antisemitism**. It had existed in Europe and around the world for centuries before World War I. Jews have often been used as **scapegoats**, **discriminated** against, driven from their homes, and even killed just for being Jewish.

Anne's dad was worried. Antisemitism was growing worse and worse. There were rumblings that another war was coming.

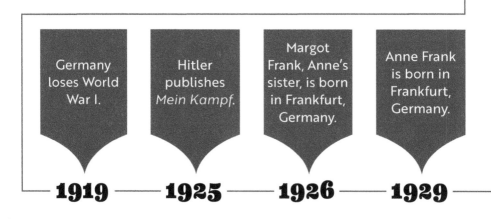

WHEN?

1919	1925	1926	1929
Germany loses World War I.	Hitler publishes *Mein Kampf.*	Margot Frank, Anne's sister, is born in Frankfurt, Germany.	Anne Frank is born in Frankfurt, Germany.

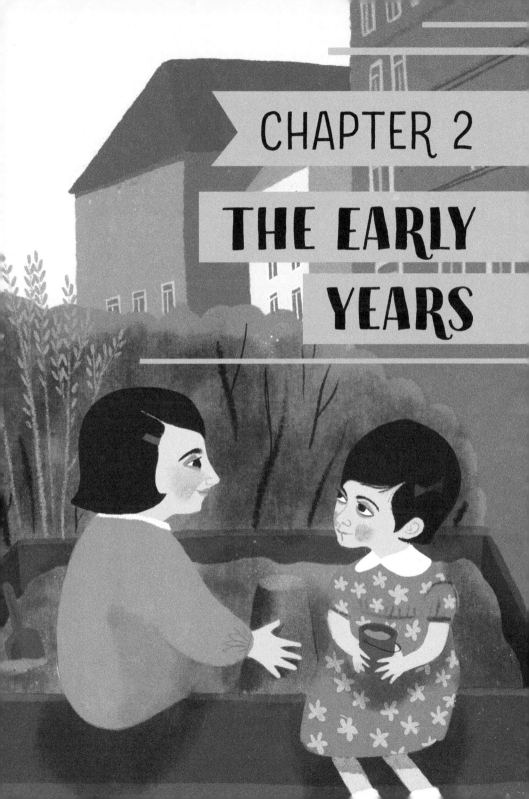

CHAPTER 2

THE EARLY YEARS

⚜ Growing Up in Germany ⚜

For Anne and Margot, their father's worries seemed far away. The sisters lived surrounded by love in their light-filled apartment in Frankfurt. Their father, whom they called "Pim," told them stories. They visited their grandmothers. Anne took naps on her parents' big bed, and when she woke up, she and Margot would play in the sandbox. Friends came over to play and eat snacks.

Anne cried a lot when she was a baby. Margot wanted to play with her, but baby Anne just screamed when she was awake. Otto would get up in the middle of the night often to rub her belly so she could go back to sleep. When Anne got a little older, she stopped crying all the time. She turned into a strong, bright, laughing toddler who loved attention. Anne liked to get her way. She'd sometimes have tantrums if she didn't.

Though their home was happy, Otto and Edith's worries grew. In January 1933, when Anne was three years old, Hitler became the leader of Germany. Quickly, he turned Germany from a **democracy** into a **dictatorship**. Hitler made all the decisions. By spring of 1933, the Nazi Party said that people in Germany were not allowed to shop at any store owned by Jews. Jewish teachers were fired from public schools. Nazis burned books by Jewish writers.

Germany was quickly growing more and more dangerous for Jews. Otto and Edith knew they might have to do something very hard to keep their daughters safe, and they were right.

✿ Fleeing Home ✿

In the summer of 1933, Otto and Edith made their decision: Germany was too dangerous for Jews. The family would move to Amsterdam, the capital of the Netherlands.

They chose Amsterdam because it was close by and Otto already spoke Dutch, the language of the Netherlands. Just as important, the Netherlands had a history of remaining **neutral** during wars. Otto thought this made it safe for his family.

THE FRANK FAMILY TREE

ABRAHAM HOLLÄNDER
1860–1927

ROSA STERN
1866–1942

MICHAEL FRANK
1851–1909

ALICE STERN
1865–1953

EDITH HOLLÄNDER
1900–1945

ANNE
1929–1945

MARGOT
1926–1945

OTTO FRANK
1889–1980

WHERE?

NETHERLANDS

GERMANY

AMSTERDAM

FRANKFURT

Otto left for Amsterdam first, and Edith soon joined him so she could look for an apartment for the Franks. Anne and Margot stayed with family. By December 1933, Edith had arranged everything and fetched Anne and Margot. After half a year, the family was together in their new home, in their new country.

Everything was different and hard. Otto started a new business. The women in the family had to learn Dutch. Margot and Anne picked it up quickly, but Edith wasn't very good at it. Compared to their home in Germany, their Dutch apartment was small. They all missed their German friends.

Lots of other Jewish families fleeing Nazi Germany had come to live in Amsterdam, too. Many lived in the same neighborhood as the Franks. Anne started going to a kindergarten nearby and made friends with a girl named Hanneli Goslar. Hanneli spoke German, too. The girls played hopscotch and hide-and-seek with the other neighborhood kids in front of the apartment building. Their parents had **Shabbat** dinner together on Fridays.

Many people of the Netherlands welcomed and helped Jewish people. They didn't believe the antisemitic messages coming from Germany. Germany and its dangerous leader were just over the border, but Jewish people were mostly safe in Amsterdam. Otto felt sure of that.

WHEN?

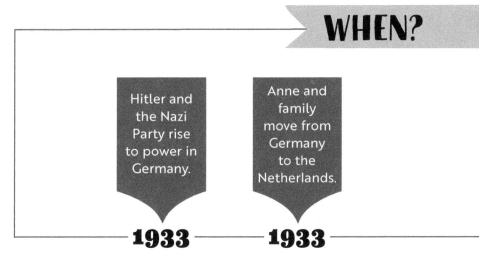

Hitler and the Nazi Party rise to power in Germany.

1933

Anne and family move from Germany to the Netherlands.

1933

CHAPTER 3

A NEW WORLD

❦ Life in Amsterdam ❧

In Amsterdam, Anne was growing into a smart, lively person. She still loved being the center of attention. She also enjoyed writing. From an early age, it became clear that she was very good at it, too.

Anne made lots of new friends in Amsterdam. They would ride their bikes together, go for ice cream after school, and play at each other's houses. Anne's house was a warm, cheerful place. Otto told stories and taught the girls silly songs. Edith served lemonade and rolls with cream cheese and chocolate bits for a snack.

> " I want to write, but more than that, I want to bring out all kinds of things that lie buried deep in my heart. "

Anne and her big sister were opposites. Margot was quiet, like her mother. She always obeyed the rules and didn't argue when she disagreed with something—not like Anne. Also unlike her sister, Anne was loud. She could be stormy or silly. Anne thought that her father understood her much better than her mother.

Meanwhile, life was growing more and more dangerous for the Jews who had stayed behind in Germany. By 1936, when Anne was seven years old, Adolf Hitler had passed more antisemitic laws. He ruled that Jewish people could not vote or marry non-Jews. The Nazis had also set up **concentration camps** as prisons for people they didn't like. The Nazis forced them to do hard labor in these camps. In 1938, they started imprisoning Jews there, just for being Jewish.

Then, on September 1, 1939, Hitler's troops **invaded** Poland. Hitler wasn't content with only controlling his own country. Now he was taking control of other countries, too. He had to be stopped. Great Britain and France declared war on Germany. World War II had begun.

Hitler Takes Over

After taking over Poland, Hitler took over Denmark and Norway. In May 1940, Hitler invaded the Netherlands. German troops now controlled Amsterdam, and Anne's life changed forever.

WHERE?

NORWAY

Land invaded by Hitler

DENMARK

NETHERLANDS

AMSTERDAM

GERMANY

POLAND

Soon after they invaded, the Nazis declared that Jews could not work as teachers or professors anymore. By January 1941, Jews had to register with the government so the Nazis could keep track of them. By February, the Nazis started rounding up some Jews and shipping them to concentration camps. By September 1941, Jews could not go to the movies or restaurants. They could not go to the beach. They were banned from visiting zoos, museums, and libraries.

Anne was furious at these **racist** and unfair laws. Still, she had to obey them. All Jews did. If they disobeyed, they could be arrested. The Franks were afraid. Still, Otto and Edith tried to keep a normal life for Anne and Margot. When Anne couldn't go to the movies for her birthday, her parents showed a movie at their house.

The United States joined World War II in December 1941. During the war, Great Britain, the Soviet Union, China, and the United States

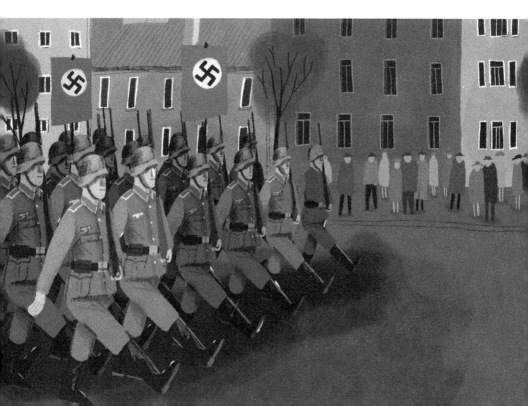

were called the **Allies**. Together, they were fighting against Germany, Italy, and Japan. Those three countries were called the **Axis** powers. Despite the Allies' growing forces, Hitler's power was growing, too.

Around this time, Hitler decided to try to kill all European Jews. He called this plan the "Final Solution." When German troops invaded a country, the Jews there would either be killed right away or sent to the concentration camps to be killed soon after. The Franks' situation grew worse every day.

WHEN?

1935	1939	1940	1941
Anne starts going to school.	Germany invades Poland. World War II begins.	Germany invades the Netherlands and takes over Amsterdam.	Jews in the Netherlands face racist, antisemitic laws.

CHAPTER 4
WORLD WAR II

⚜ **Unfair Laws** ⚜
and Yellow Stars

Anne and the Franks did not know about the Final Solution, but they knew how many new rules they had to follow just because of their religion. In May 1941, Jews could no longer go to parks. Yet another new law was passed, too: Jewish children could not go to school with Christian children. They had to go to their own school, which was called the Jewish Lyceum. Anne had to leave her school and her friends there.

Despite all of this, Anne was happy at the Jewish Lyceum. Her friend Hanneli was there also. All the teachers and students were Jewish. Everyone was struggling under Nazi rule together. The school was a warm, friendly place with excellent teachers.

Anne loved her schoolwork. Sometimes, though, she was a bit too talkative in class. One day during math class, she talked so much that her teacher gave her an assignment: She had to write an essay on what it meant to be a "**chatterbox**."

In the spring of 1942, more changes came for Anne and her classmates. All Jews now had to sew a yellow, six-pointed star on the outside of their clothes. This star was the Star of David, which was an important Jewish **symbol**. This way, the Nazis could tell immediately who was Jewish and who was not. Jews also couldn't

MYTH & FACT

Jews in Europe could escape to safer countries if they wanted to.

At the beginning of World War II, some countries allowed Jewish refugees in, but there were strict limits on how many people could enter each country. Many Jews did not get **visas** at all. Escaping became almost impossible as the war went on.

ride bicycles or take public transportation, like streetcars.

Otto and Edith desperately wanted to leave the Netherlands. They wanted to take the girls to the United States, but the United States almost never gave a visa to anyone in the Netherlands. The Franks were stuck.

⚜ **Time to Go** ⚜

Anne woke up early on June 12, 1942. It was her thirteenth birthday. She couldn't wait to get downstairs, where a very special present was waiting for her. There it was, on the table:

a diary, with a red-and-green plaid cover and a lock for privacy. Anne had picked it out herself a few days earlier.

Anne treated her diary like a friend. She called it Kitty. She told Kitty that she was going to write down all of her thoughts and feelings. And she felt sure that Kitty would always listen to her.

> So much has happened, it is just as if the whole world had turned upside down. But I am still alive, Kitty, and that is the main thing, Daddy says.

Then, on July 5, 1942, the Franks got a letter that changed their lives—again. Margot was being ordered to go to a **labor camp**. She could be worked to death, and she was only sixteen.

Otto and Edith made up their minds fast. Otto had already been planning to take his family into hiding. He had set up secret rooms for

Anne could only take a few things with her when her family went into hiding. Her diary was the most precious item she brought. What is your most precious item?

them in an **annex** behind his work building. Now was the time. They would leave the very next morning.

Anne could pack only what she could hold in her schoolbag. The family had to avoid calling attention to themselves. No one could know where they were going.

On July 6, Anne said goodbye to their cat, Moortje. She and her parents closed the door of their apartment. In a warm, early morning rain, they hurried through the Amsterdam streets. They were heading into their new, unknown life. Nothing would ever be the same again.

Anne receives a diary for her thirteenth birthday.

JUNE 12, 1942

Anne and her family go into hiding.

JULY 6, 1942

CHAPTER 5

THE SECRET ANNEX

❧ In Hiding ❧

The Franks' secret hiding place was behind Otto's warehouse and office building. From the outside, no one could tell it was there. A secret door was hidden on the landing of a second-floor staircase. When Anne saw the annex for the first time, she had to be brave.

Otto had already had food, bedding, dishes, and furniture brought into the secret annex. One of his workers had built a bathroom. The Frank family would not be hiding alone. Otto's business partner, Hermann van Pels; his wife, Auguste; and their teenage son, Peter, would be sharing the place with them. By November, a dentist named Fritz Pfeffer joined as well.

The annex had two main floors and an attic. There were two small rooms on the second floor. Margot shared one with her parents. Anne had to share the other room with Fritz, which she hated. This floor had the small bathroom.

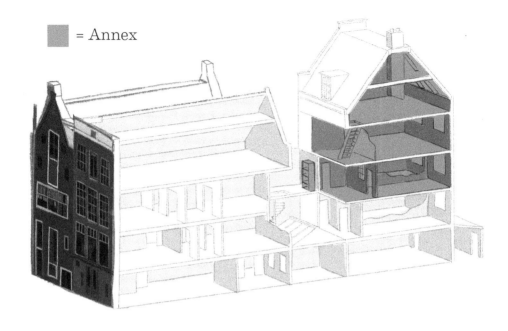

= Annex

On the third floor of the annex was one large room. This was the kitchen and the living room, and at night, it was Hermann and Auguste van Pels's bedroom. Peter slept in a tiny room off to the side.

The people in the annex could not let any of the workers in the office or the warehouse know they were there. During certain hours, they couldn't speak louder than a whisper or flush the toilet. They had to put big boards over the windows so no one outside could see their lights. Anyone who knew that Jews were hiding in the annex could have betrayed them to the Nazis.

For Anne, the outside world was gone. The annex was her entire world now.

⚘ **Anne and Kitty** ⚘

As the weeks turned to months, Anne was stuck inside the annex with many other people, day in and day out. Throughout the summer and fall of 1942, more and more Jews were being arrested and sent to concentration camps in Germany.

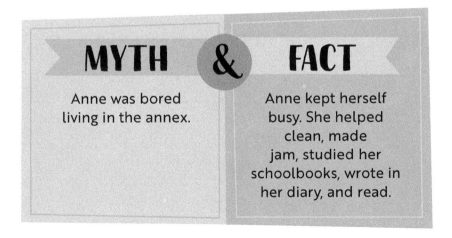

MYTH & FACT

Anne was bored living in the annex.

Anne kept herself busy. She helped clean, made jam, studied her schoolbooks, wrote in her diary, and read.

Anne was scared and cramped and sometimes annoyed. She wrote in her diary, Kitty, most days. Anne told Kitty that her mother didn't really understand her and that her father made her feel safe and loved. Her family did not treat her like an adult, she wrote. Still, they expected her to act like one.

Anne took her writing seriously. She wanted to publish her diary one day. Like any good author, Anne rewrote parts that she didn't like. She used dialogue and lots of description. Anne longed for a friend to talk to. She didn't have one in the annex, so Kitty became her best friend. Writing became her comfort.

Anne wrote about how much she hated watching Fritz, her roommate, do his exercises. She wrote about their daily fights over who could use the tiny table in their bedroom. She told Kitty that sometimes she felt overwhelmed and hopeless. Sometimes, she went into the bathroom to cry.

Outside the annex, the Allies were fighting back Hitler's forces. Seven months after the Franks went into hiding, the Allies won a big battle in the Russian city of Stalingrad.

JUMP
—IN THE—
THINK TANK

Her diary, Kitty, was Anne's best friend during her time in hiding. Think about a friend that you have. How do you and your friend support each other in hard times?

British and American forces took back Italy. Everyone in the annex listened to the radio quietly when they could. They followed the movement of the Allied troops in the newspapers.

WHEN?

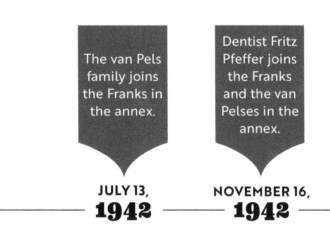

The van Pels family joins the Franks in the annex.

Dentist Fritz Pfeffer joins the Franks and the van Pelses in the annex.

JULY 13, 1942 — NOVEMBER 16, 1942

CHAPTER 6

BEHIND CLOSED DOORS

☙ Help from Outside ❧

Anne and the others weren't left totally alone in the annex. They had helpers: Otto's employees Bep Voskuijl and Miep Gies; Miep's husband, Jan; and Otto's two business partners, Johannes Kleiman and Victor Kugler. These helpers weren't Jewish, so they could still live normal lives. The helpers thought that what was happening to the Jews was wrong. They brought supplies to the Franks even though they could have been arrested if they were caught.

Visits from Miep and the other helpers were a welcome distraction in the annex. They came almost every day, usually at lunchtime. They brought magazines, news from the outside world, and, most important, food.

Anne wrote a lot about food in her diary. By the spring of 1943, it was becoming harder and harder to get certain foods. The people in the annex had to eat whatever the helpers could smuggle in without anyone's noticing. They ate a lot of beans, potatoes, vegetables, and bread. Often, they had to eat the same thing, like lettuce, for days, if that was all the helpers could get. Once, they had to eat mashed pickled kale for dinner. Anne wrote that just the thought of eating it made her feel sick.

Anne loved sugar, when they could get it. Once, the helpers were able to bring in crates of strawberries. Anne wrote they ate nothing but strawberries for days. They made jam, too, so they would have something sweet for later.

The war kept going. Anne turned fourteen in June 1943. They had been in the annex for one year.

JUMP -IN THE- THINK TANK

Helpers like Miep risked their own freedom to help the Franks. They were fighting against **injustice**. Talk about a time you stood up for something—a person, an idea, even an animal. What happened?

> 66 It's really a wonder that I haven't dropped all my ideals . . . Yet I keep them, because in spite of everything I still believe that people are really good at heart. 99

✄ **Keeping Hope Alive** ✄

By the fall of 1943, most Jews in the Netherlands had been sent to the concentration camps to die. Anne was afraid every day of being discovered by the Gestapo. Any strange noise filled her with panic. Had the Gestapo found them? Then someone familiar would come up the stairs, and everyone would relax. It was only another false alarm.

Anne and the others longed for the day when they could come out of hiding, breathe fresh air, and run around. Still, they were used to life in hiding now. Anne and Margot studied French and Latin from their schoolbooks. Anne read every novel she could get her hands on. She especially loved the movie magazines Victor would sometimes bring. She knew the names of all the actors and actresses and what movies they were starring in.

Anne still poured her heart into her diary. She wrote that she had a crush on Peter van Pels. She wrote about how she wished her mother could understand her better. She wrote that she still believed in love and beauty, even though millions of people were suffering.

By 1944, the war news was getting better. On June 6, the Allies landed on the beaches of France in the **D-Day** invasion. After they freed France, the Netherlands would not be far behind. The Franks were sure of that.

On June 12, 1944, Anne turned fifteen. She had spent two years in hiding. Perhaps she would even be able to go to school in the fall, Anne wrote in her diary. The end of the war could not be far away.

WHERE?

NETHERLANDS
AMSTERDAM
RUSSIA
NORMANDY
FRANCE
STALINGRAD
ITALY

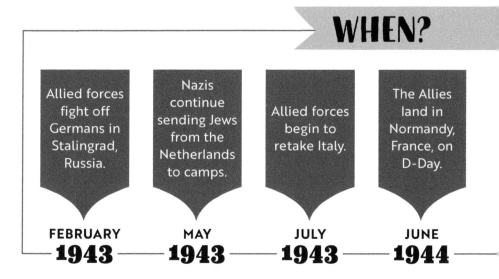

WHEN?

Allied forces fight off Germans in Stalingrad, Russia.	Nazis continue sending Jews from the Netherlands to camps.	Allied forces begin to retake Italy.	The Allies land in Normandy, France, on D-Day.
FEBRUARY **1943**	**MAY** **1943**	**JULY** **1943**	**JUNE** **1944**

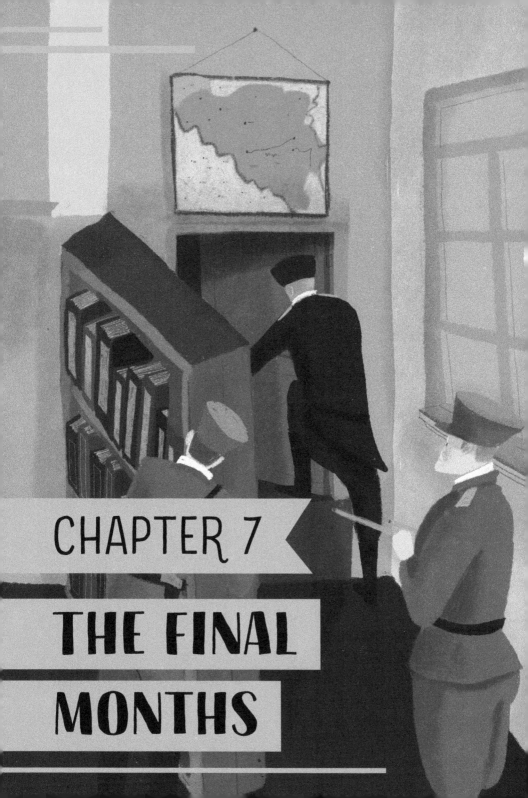

CHAPTER 7

THE FINAL MONTHS

ꙮ The Discovery ꙮ

August 4, 1944. An ordinary day in the annex. Then, suddenly, heavy footsteps on the stairs. The door was shoved open. Anne's worst nightmare had come true: The Gestapo had found them. To this day, no one knows how.

Everyone in the annex was arrested and taken away. Later, Miep went back to the empty annex. She found Kitty and carefully tucked the diary away in a drawer for safekeeping. She hoped that one day, Anne would come back for it.

Anne and the others were first sent to Westerbork, a **transit camp** in the Netherlands. Then they were sent in cattle cars to Auschwitz, a concentration camp in Poland. At Auschwitz, Anne, Edith, and Margot were separated from Otto the moment they arrived. Anne would never see her father again.

Anne's head was shaved. Her clothes were taken away. She had an ID number tattooed on the inside of her arm. Because of the dirty and crowded conditions at the camp, Anne's skin became covered with sores. She was sent to live in a special **barracks** for people with skin diseases. Some prisoners survived at Auschwitz by doing hard labor, like breaking rocks. Many more were killed.

In October 1944, four months after leaving the annex, Anne and Margot were transported again. This time, they were sent to the Bergen-Belsen concentration camp in

Germany. By then, Anne and Margot were very weak from hunger. They quickly became sick with the disease **typhus**. They lived in filthy, freezing-cold barracks. Their mother had been kept behind in Auschwitz. Anne and Margot were alone. They were dying.

🦜 **Anne's Legacy** 🦜

On April 15, 1945, British troops **liberated** Bergen-Belsen, but Anne never got to see that moment. She died of typhus sometime during February 1945, a few days after Margot. No one knows the exact date of her death. No one from her family was with her. The last words she wrote in her diary were about a future she would never have.

Germany **surrendered** on May 7, 1945, and the war was finally over. Almost everyone from the annex had died. Only Otto Frank was alive.

As soon as he could, Otto went back to Amsterdam. Miep gave him Anne's diary.

> [I] keep on trying to find a way of becoming what I would so like to be, and what I could be if . . . **there weren't any other** people living in the world.

Otto remembered that Anne had wanted to publish her diary. He could still make this dream come true.

Anne's diary was published as a book entitled *The Secret Annex*. Later, the title was changed to *Anne Frank: The Diary of a Young Girl*. Anne's powerful voice came through in her entries, and people connected with her words deeply. People from all over the globe wrote to Otto, telling him how much Anne's writing meant to them.

Her diary has been **translated** into 70 languages. Over 30 million copies of the diary have been sold.

Anne's writing still speaks to readers today. By reading Anne's diary, we can learn about the stories of the people who lived through the Holocaust and World War II. We can see how, even when facing fear and death, someone as special as Anne can be hopeful and brave.

JUMP
—IN THE—
THINK TANK

Anne wrote long ago, yet people still find meaning in her words. What do you want to tell children in the future about the time you are living in?

WHEN?

The Frank family is arrested and taken away from the secret annex.

AUGUST 4,
1944

Anne and her family are taken to Auschwitz.

SEPTEMBER 3,
1944

Anne and Margot are taken to Bergen-Belsen.

OCTOBER 30,
1944

Anne and Margot die of typhus at Bergen-Belsen.

FEBRUARY
1945

The Allies liberate Bergen-Belsen.

APRIL 15,
1945

The Germans surrender and World War II ends in Europe.

MAY 7,
1945

CHAPTER 8

SO . . . WHO WAS ANNE FRANK ?

✂ **Challenge Accepted!** ✂

You've met Anne Frank and learned about her life. Now test your knowledge! Try the quiz below. Circle the answer you think is correct. Then find the answers at the end.

1. **Where was Anne Frank born?**

→ A. Frankfurt, Germany
→ B. Amsterdam, the Netherlands
→ C. Warsaw, Poland
→ D. Vienna, Austria

2. **Who did Anne say good-bye to right before leaving her family's home to go into hiding?**

→ A. Her sister, Margot
→ B. Her friend Hanneli
→ C. Her father, Otto
→ D. Her cat, Moortje

3. **Where was the secret annex located?**

→ A. In the attic of the Franks' apartment building in Amsterdam

→ B. In the cellar of Anne's grandmother's house in Basel, Switzerland

→ C. In Otto Frank's office building in Amsterdam

→ D. In a farmhouse in the countryside in the Netherlands

4. **With whom did Anne share a room in the secret annex?**

→ A. Margot, her sister

→ B. Fritz Pfeffer, the dentist

→ C. Peter van Pels

→ D. Edith and Otto, her parents

5. **Where did Anne die?**

→ A. In the Bergen-Belsen concentration camp in Germany

→ B. In the secret annex in Amsterdam

→ C. At the Auschwitz concentration camp in Poland

→ D. In the Westerbork transit camp in the Netherlands

6. **What disease did Anne die of?**

→ A. Tuberculosis

→ B. Typhus

→ C. Diphtheria

→ D. Scabies

7. **What name did Anne call her diary?**

→ A. Puppy

→ B. Hanneli

→ C. Kitty

→ D. Dinah

8. **How old was Anne when she was arrested and taken away from the annex?**

→ A. Thirteen

→ B. Twelve

→ C. Seventeen

→ D. Fifteen

9. **Why did the Franks leave Germany and go to live in Amsterdam?**

A. Otto wanted to start a new business.

B. They had been arrested by the Nazis.

C. The Nazis were making life hard for Jews in Germany.

D. Otto and Edith were getting a divorce.

10. **What symbol did the Nazis force the Jews in Amsterdam to wear?**

A. A black armband

B. A purple belt

C. A red shirt

D. A yellow star

ꙮ Our World ꙮ

How has Anne's diary made a difference today?
Let's look at a few ways our world is better
because of Anne's words:

→ Anne's diary is read by kids in schools across the
globe. Teachers use Anne's diary to teach kids about
the Holocaust, so we can make sure that the mistakes
of the past are never repeated.

→ The secret annex is now a museum called the Anne
Frank House. The museum runs programs about **justice**
and **tolerance**. Every year, 1.2 million people visit so they
can learn more about Anne's life and the lives of all Jews
during the Holocaust.

→ Organizations all over the world use Anne's **legacy**
to inspire **humanitarian** work. The Anne Frank
Trust UK works to fight prejudice in young people.
The Anne Frank Center for Mutual Respect provides
arts programming and education aimed at creating a
kinder world.

MORE!

Let's think more about Anne's writing, what she wanted to see in the world, and how our own lives are similar to or different from Anne's.

→ If Anne was alive today and you could ask her any question you wanted, what would you ask and why?

→ Think of one way Anne's diary can inspire you to make a change in your own life. What would that change be?

→ What is one way our world today is similar to Anne's world? What is one way our world is different?

Glossary

Allies: The group of countries fighting against Germany during World War II, including the United States, Great Britain, France, the Soviet Union, and China

annex: A space or building joined to another building

antisemitism: The act of disliking people or treating them unfairly because they are Jewish

Axis: Germany and the countries fighting on its side during World War II, including Italy and Japan

barracks: A group of buildings for prisoners, soldiers, or laborers to live in

chatterbox: A person who talks a lot

concentration camp: A place where large numbers of people are imprisoned without good food, water, clothing, or space

D-Day: June 6, 1944; the day on which the Allies invaded northern France to try to liberate it from the Nazis

democracy: A type of government in which everyone participates by electing leaders

dictatorship: A type of government in which one leader makes all the decisions and controls all the power

discriminate: To treat someone unfairly or differently because of their race, sex, religion, or age

Gestapo: The secret police of Nazi Germany

Holocaust: The mass killing of more than six million Jewish people and millions of others by Hitler's Nazis in Europe during World War II (1941 to 1945)

humanitarian: Promoting the welfare of people and making their lives better

injustice: Unfairness

invade: To occupy a country and take it over by force

Jewish: A word used to describe a person who follows the religion of Judaism or who identifies culturally with the Jewish people

justice: Fairness

labor camp: A prison camp in which people are forced to do hard work

legacy: One's lasting influence on other people

liberate: To free from confinement

Nazi: A member of the National Socialist German Workers' Party, led by Adolf Hitler

neutral: Not supporting one side or the other in a conflict

political: Something related to politics, the art and science of government

prejudice: Disliking a person or group without any logical reason

racist: Discriminating against someone of a different race based on the belief that one's own race is superior

scapegoat: Someone who is blamed for something they didn't do or cause

Shabbat: The Jewish Sabbath, or day of rest and prayer, beginning on Friday night and ending on Saturday night

SS (Schutzstaffel): The Nazi police

surrender: To give up against an opponent

symbol: A sign or object that stands for something

tolerance: Accepting people whose beliefs or practices are different from one's own

transit camp: A camp for groups of people moving or being moved to a different place

translate: To change words from one language to another

typhus: A dangerous infectious disease that causes a fever, rash, and hallucinations, spread through ticks, fleas, and lice

visa: An official document that allows people to enter, stay in, or leave a country for a certain reason and amount of time

World War I: A war that lasted from 1914 to 1918 and was fought mainly between the Allies (the United States, Great Britain, France, Russia, and Italy) and the Central Powers (Germany, Austria-Hungary, Bulgaria, and the Ottoman Empire)

World War II: A war that lasted from 1939 to 1945 and was fought mainly between the Allies (the United States, Great Britain, France, the Soviet Union, and China) and the Axis (Germany, Italy, and Japan)

Bibliography

Anne Frank House. "The Secret Annex." AnneFrank.org/en/anne-frank /secret-annex.

Anne Frank House. "The Timeline." AnneFrank.org/en/anne-frank /the-timeline.

Anne Frank House. "Who Was Anne Frank?" AnneFrank.org/en/anne -frank/who-was-anne-frank.

Frank, Anne. *Anne Frank: The Diary of a Young Girl*. New York: Pocket Books, 1958.

Imperial War Museums. "The Liberation of Bergen-Belsen." IWM.org.uk /history/the-liberation-of-bergen-belsen.

Molloy, Annette. "Anne Frank's Childhood Friend Tells of Their Traumatic Final Meeting at Bergen-Belsen and Says the Teenager 'Always Wanted to Be Heard.'" *Independent*, March 10, 2015. independent.co.uk/news/people /anne-franks-childhood-friend-tells-of-their-traumatic-final-meeting-at -bergen-belsen-and-says-the-10098632.html.

Müller, Melissa. *Anne Frank: The Biography*. New York: Metropolitan Books, 2013.

Ozick, Cynthia. "Who Owns Anne Frank?" *New Yorker*, September 29, 1997. NewYorker.com/magazine/1997/10/06/who-owns-anne-frank.

Prins, Erika, and Gertjan Broek. "One Day They Simply Weren't There Any More." Anne Frank House, March 2015. AnneFrank.org/en/downloads /filer_public/08/b3/08b3ff12-d8c1-4964-b9ec-e17a7b035a76/one_day_they _simply_weren.pdf.

Prose, Francine. *Anne Frank: The Book, the Life, the Afterlife*. New York: HarperCollins, 2009.

United States Holocaust Memorial Museum. "Anne Frank Biography." Holocaust Encyclopedia. Encyclopedia.USHMM.org/content/en/article /anne-frank-biography.

United States Holocaust Memorial Museum. "Final Solution: Overview." Holocaust Encyclopedia. Encyclopedia.USHMM.org/content/en/article /final-solution-overview.

Winter, Michael. "New Research Sets Anne Frank's Death Earlier." *USA Today*, March 31, 2015. USAToday.com/story/news/2015/03/31/anne-frank -death-probably-february-1945/70742898.

Worland, Justin. "Anne Frank's Diary Now Has a Co-Author to Extend Copyright." *Time*, November 15, 2015. Time.com/4113855/anne-frank-diary -co-author.

Acknowledgments

I am deeply grateful to the Anne Frank House in Amsterdam, the Netherlands. This museum preserves the secret annex and provides a wealth of information about Anne's life and the history surrounding it. I drew on this material many times, including the virtual tour of the annex itself. I'd also like to thank my editor, Orli Zuravicky, who gave me the chance to examine Anne's life and provided such smart feedback. And finally, I would like to express my gratitude to freedom fighters everywhere. Reading and writing about Anne's experiences has been chilling at times but has strengthened my resolve that my own country should never follow the path of Nazi Germany. To defend our own democracy would be the finest tribute to Anne's legacy.

About the Author

EMMA CARLSON BERNE has written many books for young people, including *A Hanukkah Celebration* (Rockridge Press, 2020) and *Books by Horseback* (Little Bee, 2021). Emma often writes on topics related to Jewish life, history, and culture and has previously published titles on Kristallnacht and the Kindertransport. As a Jewish person, Emma welcomes the chance to explore these periods in her people's history.

Emma lives in Cincinnati, Ohio, where she often visits schools to speak about writing and the life of an author. Emma enjoys horseback riding, hiking, camping, and cooking. She is the mother of three boys and two cat-children. More about Emma and her books can be found at EmmaCarlsonBerne.com.

About the Illustrator

ANNITA SOBLE's illustrations have appeared in a wide array of media, including magazines, greeting cards, and animations. She lives with her husband and their five children in Brooklyn, New York.

WHO WILL INSPIRE YOU NEXT?

EXPLORE A WORLD OF HEROES AND ROLE MODELS IN
THE STORY OF... BIOGRAPHY SERIES FOR NEW READERS.

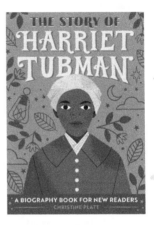

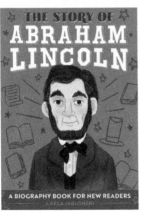

LOOK FOR THIS SERIES
WHEREVER BOOKS AND EBOOKS ARE SOLD

Alexander Hamilton

Albert Einstein

Martin Luther King Jr.

George Washington

Jane Goodall

Barack Obama

Helen Keller

Marie Curie

CPSIA information can be obtained
at www.ICGtesting.com
Printed in the USA
JSHW050232130221
11830JS00006B/8